Cover and Interior Illustrations by Donella Frampton

AuthorHouse™ UK
1663 Liberty Drive
Bloomington, IN 47403 USA
www.authorhouse.co.uk
Phone: 0800 047 8203 (Domestic TFN)
+44 1908 723714 (International)

Because of the dynamic nature of the Internet, any web addresses or links contained in this book may have changed since publication and may no longer be valid. The views expressed in this work are solely those of the author and do not necessarily reflect the views of the publisher, and the publisher hereby disclaims any responsibility for them.

This book is printed on acid-free paper.

ISBN: 978-1-7283-9214-1 (sc)
ISBN: 978-1-7283-9213-4 (e)

Print information available on the last page.

Published by AuthorHouse 10/31/2019

authorHOUSE

About the Book

If you coach an under 5's or under 6's football team or you are the chairman of a club with an under 5's or under 6's team, then this book was written for you.

I've worked with players aged 2-6 for the last 10 years and experienced just about everything there is to see, although no two sessions with this age group are alike. You'll see in this book I'm absolutely committed to providing children a lasting positive impact through Love, Learning & Laughing. I'm passionate about Learning — Learning makes our players happy. I truly believe in the transformative power of Laughing and feeling Loved and their ability to engage children, promote positivity and build lasting relationships that empower and inspire children.

Contents

About the Book iii

Introduction 1

Philosophy... 1

The Child... 1

Equipment Needed 1

Curriculum Structure 2

Basic Skills 2

How to use these sessions.. 2

Spring 4

What's Next?.. 44

Have you read our other books?... 44

U7's-U11's Foundation Phase 44

Academy Soccer Coach... 44

Secret Marketing Strategy 45

About the Author... 47

THE COMPLETE SERIES TO COACHING 4-6 YEAR OLDS

v

Introduction

If you coach children aged 4-6, coach in an under 5's or under 6's football team or you are the chairman of a club with an under 5's and 6's team, then this series of books was written for you.

I've worked with players aged 2-6 for the last 10 years and experienced just about everything there is to see, although no two sessions with this age group are alike. You'll see in this book I'm absolutely committed to providing children a lasting positive impact through Love, Learning & Laughing. I'm passionate about Learning — Learning makes our players happy. I truly believe in the transformative power of Laughing and feeling Loved and their ability to engage children, promote positivity and build lasting relationships that empower and inspire children.

Philosophy

My structure is built upon three core components. These components are the building blocks of the curriculum.

- **Love**— Inspire – Care for each player so that they never forget how special we made them feel. We can use football to engage and inspire young players to build better lives for themselves, helping them to realise their own self-worth. I think this programme can position a player for a lifetime of success in and out of football.
- **Learning**— Repetition - Deliberate practice is the key to learning. To master new skills, players need to receive a high frequency of realistic situations that offer maximum ball contact. Players practice ball moves over and over again so that they become natural and in turn, perform the skill quicker. This leads to them feeling proud of their learning and pride comes from mastery.
- **Laughing**— Positivity - During football sharing becomes easy, communication flows, rules are followed, and decisions are made easily. Sharing fun leads to making new friends, they challenge us and increase our learning. Childhood is a critical time for us coaches to influence positivity on our players. We welcome players of all abilities with open arms and teach them a fun, healthy game. By mastering the basic skills early on they should go on to play for the rest of their lives.

The Child

4-6-year olds are naturally selfish with the ball so we encourage dribbling techniques which they can develop without pressure and then we effectively turn those techniques into skills during fun little competitive games which will become a powerful attribute for them to use and gain confidence on the pitch. The curriculum focuses on teaching the fundamentals in a fun based play environment that involves engaging their imagination by telling stories. They will have lots of touches of the football with our ball mastery practices which includes 1 ball per child.

Johan Cruyff - "Football has to be fun for kids or it doesn't make sense".

Equipment Needed

1 ball per player (Max 12 players in a group).

20 White, Red, Green, Blue & Yellow Cones.

10 Red, Blue, Green, Orange & Yellow Witch Hat Cones.

2-4 Pop-Up Nets.

Curriculum Structure

The curriculum is targeted to players aged 4 - 6 years old. From my experience a player who is just starting out needs to immediately experience the fun aspect of the game. Therefore, this curriculum focuses on teaching the fundamentals in a fun based play environment. At a young age, mastery of the ball is vital for a child's future development. Players focus on technique and skill development.

The curriculum follows a researched and proven approach to player development and each session has a fun story/theme and focuses on one of 7 basic skills. All sessions have the same structure. The following information introduces my coaching method:

Ball Mastery – This activity gives young players an opportunity to take control of their own ball; one ball per player helps rapidly improve technique and in turn builds more confidence in dribbling. The focus is to maximise ball contact. This takes place during the first 10 minutes of the session.

Technique – This is the next 10 minutes of the session and allows players to develop the basic techniques without the threat of being tackled constantly, this part is unopposed or a light challenge such as 4 attackers vs 1 defender. Competition is added in the form of racing to add an element of pressure however it's not 1v1. Players will still have their own ball in most technique sessions.

Skill – The next 10 minutes focuses on mastering the basic skill of the session. Players must use the technique learnt in a 1v1 situation or game-like situation. Players will not have a ball each during the skill part of the session.

Matches – Every session should finish with a small-sided game no more than 3v3. These matches allow you to start teaching the basic rules of the games such as no hands, only one player at a time is allowed to leave the pitch to retrieve the ball for a throw-in. Try to allow the game to flow as much as possible only intervening for handball's, allow a lot of 'fouls' to flow and play on. This is the time for players to show what they have learnt and express themselves. About 30 minutes in length.

Basic Skills

Our goal is to support their development into their first junior football team. Focus on these basic skills;

1. Controlling the ball with both feet.
2. Controlling the ball with the sole of both feet.
3. Moving left & right with the ball.
4. Moving forward with the ball & stopping.
5. Turning & tricks.
6. Protecting the ball.
7. Shooting.

How to use these sessions

The books are split into the 4 seasons and each season has 13 weeks; each book has 13 games. Some games in a season are random like pirates or dinosaurs but most are in there because they fit the season and model with what our players are learning at school like penguins in the winter or gardening in the spring. The final book also has 13 games and features something for all seasons; this can be used as an additional learning resource and features some of the children's favourite themes like Zombies, Rockstar's and Superheroes. These sessions are built around football skills but are also an education into the real world for some children. You won't see anything in this book that looks like the adult's game because this book is designed to be age-appropriate for children.

Spring

World Book Day – 5-7

St. Patrick's Day – 8-10

Mother's Day – 11-13

Sports Relief – 14-16

Horses (Grand National) – 17-19

Gardening – 20-22

Easter – 23-25

Firefighters – 26-28

The Queen's Birthday – 29-31

Galaxy Combat – 32-34

What Time Is It? – 35-37

Battleships – 38-40

Camping – 41-43

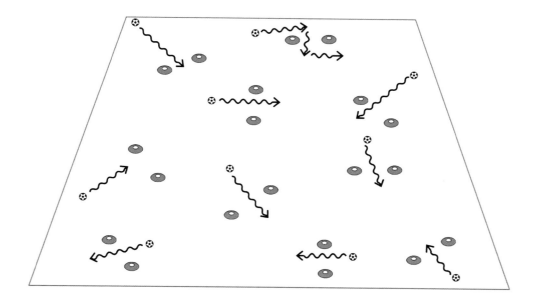

World Book Day – Turning & Tricks – Ball Mastery

This game is all about World Book Day. We will be working on Turning & Tricks. Why do we need to Turn? Protect the ball. Why do we need to do Tricks? Beat a Defender.

Organisation:

1. Footballs 2. Goals 3. Bibs 4. 20 Red Cones 5. 24 Blue Cones

Story/Description:

1. Horrid Henry is a silly prankster who is always playing tricks, we're going to do tricks too.
2. The Players dribble to a gate and do a trick through it e.g. Feints, Stepovers or do a turn and dribble away.

Coaching Points:

1. Coach demonstrates tricks/turns
2. Look around to avoid using the same gate as another player
3. Speed up when you can 4. Use different parts of the foot

Developments:

1. The coach can ask players to demo a trick or turn
2. The Players use all parts of the foot and as many different tricks and turns they can think of… Rolls, Drag backs, Stepovers & Chops/Cuts.

World Book Day – Turning & Tricks – Technique

This game is all about World Book Day. We will be working on Turning & Tricks. Why do we need to Turn? Protect the ball. Why do we need to do Tricks? Beat a Defender.

Organisation:

1. Footballs 2. Goals 3. Bibs 4. 20 Red Cones 5. 24 Blue Cones

Story/Description:

1. Players pair up - ball each. One is Horrid Henry and the other is Perfect Peter (Henry's Brother).
2. Perfect Peter tries to play with Horrid Henry, but Henry does tricks on him and dribbles away.

Coaching Points:

1. Coach demonstrates tricks/turns
2. Look around to dribble into space left by others to avoid Peter catching Henry
3. Speed up when you can
4. Use different parts of the foot

Developments:

1. Play initially until coach shouts 'Swop' and the players swop roles.
2. Progress to swopping every time Henry is caught or Henry dribbles out of area.
3. Challenge some players not to tackle Henry but try to force them to dribble out the area before swopping.

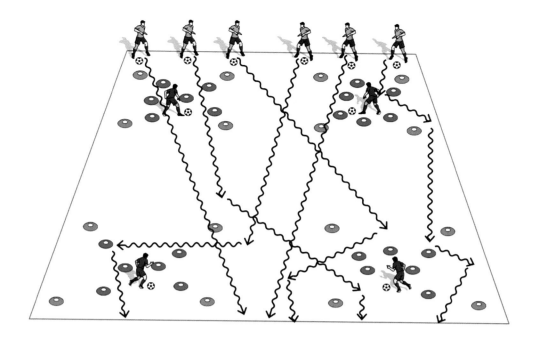

World Book Day – Turning & Tricks – Skill

This game is all about World Book Day. We will be working on Turning & Tricks. Why do we need to Turn? Protect the ball. Why do we need to do Tricks? Beat a Defender.

Organisation:

1. Footballs 2. Goals 3. Bibs 4. 20 Red Cones 5. 24 Blue Cones

Story/Description:

1. Four Perfect Peter's play nicely in their bedroom. Dribbling in & out of 6 cones inside red box.
2. Horrid Henry's dribble across area also dribbling in & out of Perfect Peter's room teasing him.
3. Perfect Peter's attempt to tag Horrid Henry's as they dribble through the room.

Coaching Points:

1. Coach demonstrates tricks/turns
2. Talk briefly about the decisions the players have when entering Perfect Peter's room, so players can successfully dribble through without being tagged
3. Speed up when you can
4. Use different parts of the foot

Developments:

1. Play for a set amount of time then swop Perfect Peter's or just swop after every successful tag
2. If players are low on ability or confidence allow them to dribble across without entering the red areas but encourage them to take a risk and praise them enormously if they do.

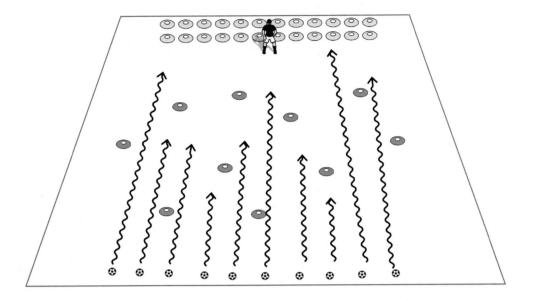

St. Patrick's Day – Controlling the ball with both feet – Ball Mastery

Our game is all about St. Patrick's Day. We will be working on controlling the ball with both feet. We need to master using both feet so that we have control of the ball always and feel comfortable in any situation like scoring a goal or passing to our friends.

Organisation:

1. Footballs 2. Goals 3. Bibs 4. 10 Green Cones 5. Yellow Cones 5. 4 Yellow WH Cones 6. 4 White, Blue & Red Cones

Story/Description:

1. The players are Leprechauns.
2. Leprechauns dribble through the forest & steal 1 piece of gold for their pots.
3. The coach turns around and players stop their ball & freeze.
4. Once collected a piece of gold take it back to starting point as quick as they can.

Coaching Points:

1. Players attempt to use both feet whilst dribbling in and out of forest.

Developments:

1. Coach can chase Leprechaun's they should learn to protect the ball or trick the coach.

CHRIS HUGHES

8

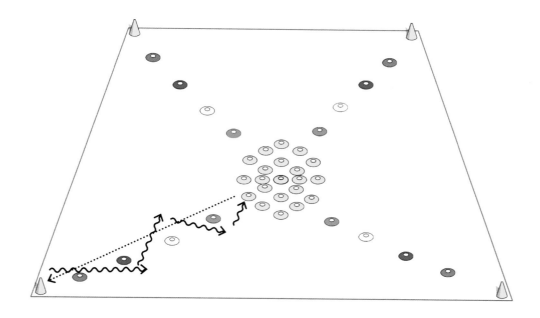

St. Patrick's Day – Controlling the ball with both feet – Technique

Our game is all about St. Patrick's Day. We will be working on controlling the ball with both feet. We need to master using both feet so that we have control of the ball always and feel comfortable in any situation like scoring a goal or passing to our friends.

Organisation:

1. Footballs 2. Goals 3. Bibs 4. 10 Green Cones 5. Yellow Cones 5. 4 Yellow WH Cones 6. 4 White, Blue & Red Cones

Story/Description:

1. The players are Leprechauns.
2. Leprechauns run in & out the rainbow and collect 1 piece of gold for their pots.
3. When all gold collected, count each team's Pot of Gold & see who has the most. Decide on winners then play again.

Coaching Points:

1. Players attempt to use both feet whilst dribbling in and out.

Developments:

1. If you bump into a cone you must leave gold and head back to your pot.

9

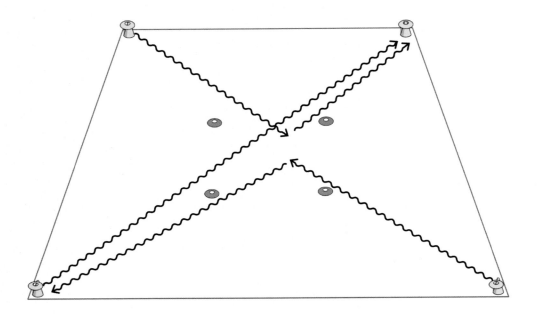

St. Patrick's Day – Controlling the ball with both feet – Skill

Our game is all about St. Patrick's Day. We will be working on controlling the ball with both feet. We need to master using both feet so that we have control of the ball always and feel comfortable in any situation like scoring a goal or passing to our friends.

Organisation:

1. Footballs 2. Goals 3. Bibs 4. 10 Green Cones 5. Yellow Cones 5. 4 Yellow WH Cones 6. 4 White, Blue & Red Cones.

Story/Description:

1. The players are Leprechauns.
2. Leprechauns are now going to dribble through the emerald forest and steal from the other Leprechauns Pots of Gold.
3. When all gold collected, count each team's Pot of Gold & see who has the most. Decide on winners then play again.

Coaching Points:

1. Players attempt to use both feet whilst dribbling in and out. Keep head up & don't bump into other players.

Developments:

1. If you bump into another player must go back and start again 2. Can steal 2 pieces of gold at a time but must leave one in the emerald forest, try to time leaving it so a teammate can collect it for a quicker steal.

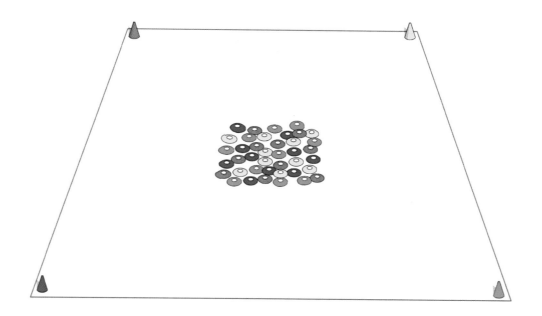

Mother's Day – Sole of the Foot – Ball Mastery

Our game is all about Mother's Day. We will be working on controlling the ball with the Sole of our Foot. Why do we need to master using the Sole of the Foot? To stop the ball. Why else might we use the sole of the foot? To tease and trick the defender.

Organisation:

1. Footballs 2. Goals 3. Bibs 4. 10-20 Cones in Yellow, Green, Red & Blue. 5. 4 Witch Hat Cones in Yellow, Green, Red & Blue.

Story/Description:

1. The players are collecting gifts (Blue- Chocolates, Yellow- Flowers, Green- Surprises, Red- Cards) for their Mothers.
2. The players must collect gifts from the middle of the room and take them to the corresponding cone in the corner; stop the ball with sole of foot.

Coaching Points:

1. Use sole of foot to avoid other players. 2. Speed up when you can.

Developments:

1. Use the sole to roll the ball from side to side whilst moving around other players.

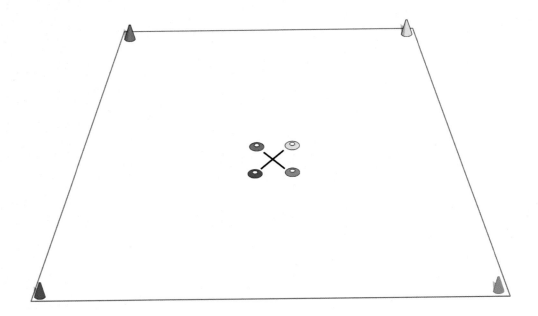

Mother's Day – Sole of the Foot – Technique

Our game is all about Mother's Day. We will be working on controlling the ball with the Sole of our Foot. Why do we need to master using the Sole of the Foot? To stop the ball. Why else might we use the sole of the foot? To tease and trick the defender.

Organisation:

1. Footballs 2. Goals 3. Bibs 4. 10-20 Cones in Yellow, Green, Red & Blue. 5. 4 Witch Hat Cones in Yellow, Green, Red & Blue.

Story/Description:

1. The players collect one of each gift from the 4 corners
2. The players then layout a square & stand inside it
3. The coach then shouts one of the gifts 'Cards' & players use sole to roll ball in that direction
4. Repeat but this time players dribble around the outside of the cone and back into the middle.

Coaching Points:

1. Try to move a meter in each direction. Players can touch the ball more than once to do this
2. Speed up when you can
3. Place arms out to keep balance and learn to protect the ball

Developments:

1. Coach shouts 2 or 3 gifts and players move towards them in order
2. Learning to shift the ball and body weight whilst keeping foot on the ball.

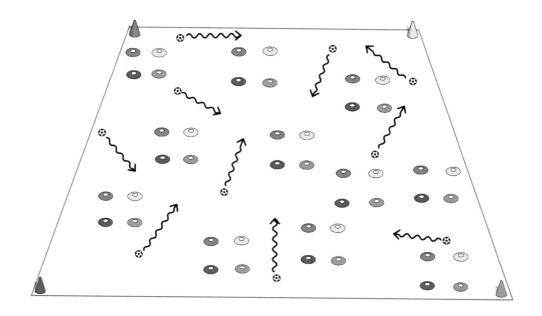

Mother's Day – Sole of the Foot – Skill

Our game is all about Mother's Day. We will be working on controlling the ball with the Sole of our Foot. Why do we need to master using the Sole of the Foot? To stop the ball. Why else might we use the sole of the foot? To tease and trick the defender.

Organisation:

1. Footballs 2. Goals 3. Bibs 4. 10-20 Cones in Yellow, Green, Red & Blue. 5. 4 Witch Hat Cones in Yellow, Green, Red & Blue.

Story/Description:

1. The players dribble avoiding shops.
2. Coach shouts 'Shops' & players dribble to an empty shop and wait for the coach to shout which gift to move towards.
3. Repeat.

Coaching Points:

1. Try to move a meter in each direction. Players can touch the ball more than once to do this
2. Speed up when you can.
3. Place arms out to keep balance and learn to protect the ball.

Developments:

1. Remove some shops so it's a race to find an empty shop
2. Coach becomes thief and wants to steal their gifts; players decide when to enter the shops to hide safely from the thief. Once the thief leaves, players must dribble away but keep looking for danger.

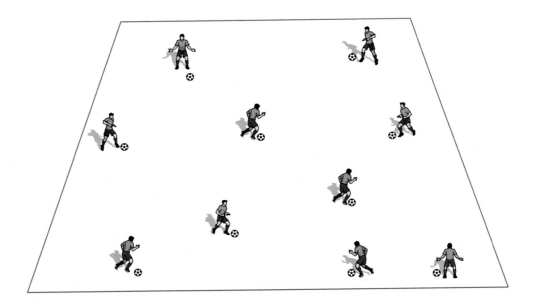

Sport Relief – Controlling the ball with both feet – Ball Mastery

Today is Sport Relief this is when the British public get active and have fun to help change lives. We're going to take part in a circuit class: We will be working on all seven steps to becoming the greatest footballer ever.

Organisation:

1. Footballs 2. Goals 3. Bibs

Story/Description:

1. Footballers need to be healthy (Dribble ball around the area).
2. Footballers need strong legs (Hands on Hips, Ball in between legs, Squats; count to ten).
3. Dribble around the area again.
4. Footballers need good balance (Stand on one Leg, hold ball, hopping; count to 10 - swop legs & count again).
5. Dribble around the room again.
6. Footballers need big muscles (Tense arms- Do ten press ups).

Coaching Points:

1. Players attempt to use both feet whilst dribbling around the area.

Developments:

1. Coach should give individual challenges to players excelling.

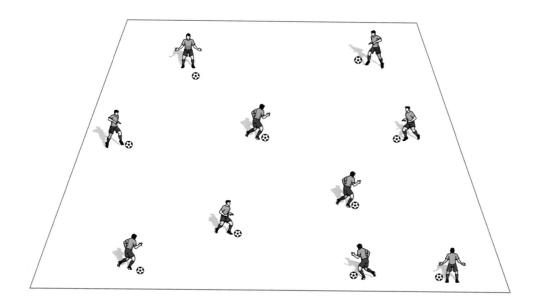

Sport Relief – 6 Ball Mastery Moves – Technique

Today is Sport Relief this is when the British public get active and have fun to help change lives. We're going to take part in a circuit class: We will be working on all seven steps to becoming the greatest footballer ever.

Organisation:

1. Footballs 2. Goals 3. Bibs

Story/Description: Players dribble around coach shouts out ball move, gives demo and players repeat.

1. Sole of the foot – Roll ball forwards & Backwards.
2. Use both feet – Pass ball between feet.
3. Drop & Stops – Pick ball up drop it and stop it.
4. Turning – Sole of foot on ball, roll it backwards and chase.
5. Step Overs- Stand still make a circle above the ball.
6. Protecting the ball – Coach chases the players who turn around to protect the ball.

Coaching Points:

1. Players attempt to use both feet whilst dribbling around the area.

Developments:

1. Coach should give individual challenges to players excelling.

Sport Relief – 6 Ball Mastery Moves – Skill

Today is Sport Relief this is when the British public get active and have fun to help change lives. We're going to take part in a circuit class: We will be working on all seven steps to becoming the greatest footballer ever.

Organisation:

1. Footballs 2. Goals 3. Bibs

Story/Description: Players dribble around coach shouts out ball movement and players react to instruction as quickly as possible.

1. Sole of the foot – Roll ball forward, backwards & even sideways whilst dribbling.
2. Use both feet – Pass ball between feet.
3. Drop & Stops – Pick ball up drop it and stop it.
4. Turn – Sole of foot on ball, roll it backwards and chase.
5. Step Overs- Step-over whilst ball is rolling.
6. Protect the ball – Coach shouts protect. The players turn their back to the coach to protect the ball – coach can move still players must react to this.

Coaching Points:

1. Use other foot when doing Drop & Stops to stop ball.

Developments:

1. Coach should give individual challenges to players excelling.

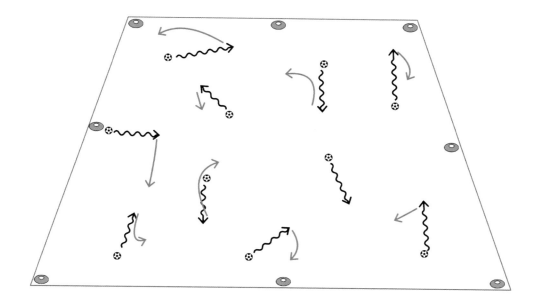

Horses – Grand National – Protecting the Ball – Ball Mastery

This game is all about The Grand National; The biggest horse race in England. We will be working on Protecting the Ball. Why do we need to protect the ball? To keep it away from Defenders and keep it for our team.

Organisation:

1. Footballs 2. Goals 3. Bibs 4. 6 Yellow, Blue & Red cones. 5. Lots of green cones.

Story/Description:

1. The Players are training their Horse for the race.
2. They keep the Reins (Football) close so the Horse doesn't run away.
3. The Coach shouts 'Yee-Haw' and it scares the players horses. Players must turn or dribble away from the coach and protect their horse. When the coach gets close players can use the sole of their foot and their body position to protect the horse.

Coaching Points:

1. Where is the Danger? Coach; Look at the coach
2. Where is the Football? At player's feet; Feel the ball don't look at the ball.

Developments:

1. Designated Player can shout 'Yee-haw' instead of coach.

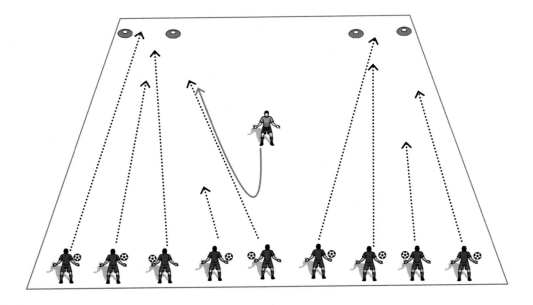

Horses – Grand National – Protecting the Ball – Technique

This game is all about The Grand National; The biggest horse race in England. We will be working on Protecting the Ball. Why do we need to protect the ball? To keep it away from Defenders and keep it for our team.

Organisation:

1. Footballs 2. Goals 3. Bibs 4. 6 Yellow, Blue & Red cones. 5. Lots of green cones.

Story/Description:

1. Somebody has let all the horses (Players) out of the stables and left the field gates open.
2. It is the Horse Trainers (Coach) task to catch all the horses before they escape by grabbing the reins (Touching their football).
3. If the Horse Trainer catches you, you become a Horse Trainer too.
4. Horses run from the back of the field and try to escape out of one of the two gates.
5. Players carry the ball under favoured arm and use their other arm to protect the ball.

Coaching Points:

1. Where is the Danger? Coach; Look at the coach
2. Where is the Football? Feel the ball don't look at the ball.
3. Twist and turn when running to keep body in the way of the ball.

Developments:

1. Play without the ball once or twice to show players how body positioning can protect their ball.
2. Play with ball at the foot (Coach tackles and players become Horse Trainers too).

CHRIS HUGHES

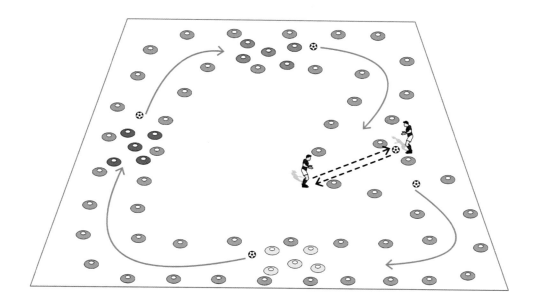

Horses – Grand National – Protecting the Ball – Skill

This game is all about The Grand National; The biggest horse race in England. We will be working on Protecting the Ball. Why do we need to protect the ball? To keep it away from Defenders and keep it for our team.

Organisation:

1. Footballs 2. Goals 3. Bibs 4. 6 Yellow, Blue & Red cones. 5. Lots of green cones.

Story/Description:

1. The Players are taking part in the Grand National Race. On the coach's command, players set off to complete circuit.
2. Sand Pits (Yellow Cones), Water Features (Blue Cones) and Valentines Ditch (Red Cones) are all part of the hazards.
3. Coach watches for horses falling off the track, if they do they become a wild horse. (Wild Horse pass football back and forth).
4. Find and crown winner!

Coaching Points:

1. Protect the horse (Football) from falling off the track.
2. Timing of pass to not hit other horses still racing.
3. Head up to watch for hazards including moving Wild Horses.

Developments:

1. Coach/Assistant/Parent can join in with 1st, 3rd, 5th Wild horse etc.

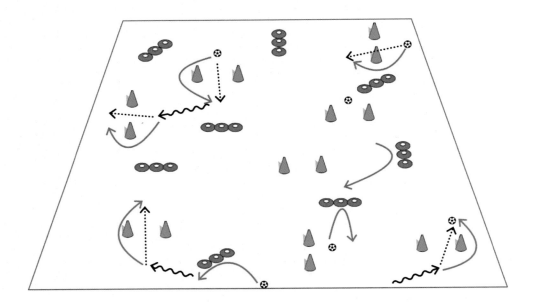

Gardening – Turning & Tricks – Ball Mastery

This game is all about Gardening. We will be working on Turning & Tricks. Why do we need to Turn? Protect the ball. Why do we need to do Tricks? Beat a Defender.

Organisation:

1. Footballs 2. Goals 3. Bibs 4. Green WH Cones 5. Red Cones

Story/Description:

1. The Players are Gardening. They must turn at the Fence Panels (Red Cones) and dribble straight through the Greenhouses (Green WH Cones).

Coaching Points:

1. Keep head up, don't bump into other Gardeners.
2. Use Sole of foot to stop the ball hitting the fence.
3. Use Sole of foot to control ball through the Greenhouses.

Developments:

1. Teach and/or Challenge players to use different skills when passing through the Greenhouses I.e. Feints, Dummy's, Shimmy's.
2. Teach and/or Challenge players to use different turns when approaching the Fence Panels I.e. Sole of the foot (Drag backs), Outside & Inside (Chops & Cuts).

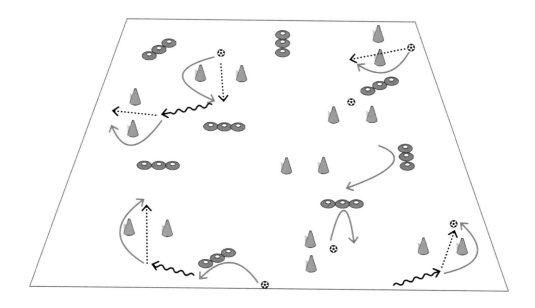

Gardening – Turning & Tricks – Technique

This game is all about Gardening. We will be working on Turning & Tricks. Why do we need to Turn? Protect the ball. Why do we need to do Tricks? Beat a Defender.

Organisation:

1. Footballs 2. Goals 3. Bibs 4. Green WH Cones 5. Red Cones

Story/Description:

1. The Players are Gardening. They must turn at the Fence Panels (Red Cones) and dribble through the Greenhouses (Green WH Cones).
2. Players learn to 'Drop Shoulder' by dribbling to the Greenhouses – nudging the ball through, running around the outside and collecting the football on the other side.
3. Player learn the 'V Drag Back' by dribbling at and turning away from the Fence Panels – dragging the ball back in and pushing it out the other way like the letter V.

Coaching Points:

1. Keep head up, don't bump into other Gardeners.
2. Use Sole of foot to stop the ball hitting the fence.
3. Coach the disguise in the skill and the importance of tricking the defender.

Developments:

1. Teach and/or Challenge players to use different skills when passing through the Greenhouses I.e. Feints, Dummy's, Shimmy's.
2. Teach and/or Challenge players to use different turns when approaching the Fence Panels I.e. Sole of the foot (Drag backs), Outside & Inside (Chops & Cuts).

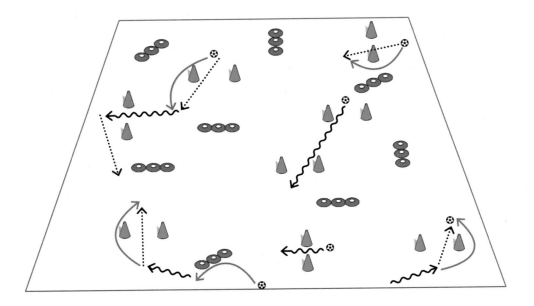

Gardening – Turning & Tricks – Skill

This game is all about Gardening. We will be working on Turning & Tricks. Why do we need to Turn? Protect the ball. Why do we need to do Tricks? Beat a Defender.

Organisation:

1. Footballs 2. Goals 3. Bibs 4. Green WH Cones 5. Red Cones

Story/Description:

1. The Players are Gardening. They must turn at the Fence Panels (Red Cones) and dribble through the Greenhouses (Green WH Cones).
2. Players dribble through and turn at as many Greenhouses & Fence Panels as possible in a minute- Keep your own score, play again try to beat own score.
3. Players compete against each other, Keep their own score and find out who the winner is.

Coaching Points:

1. Keep head up, don't bump into other Gardeners.
2. Use Sole of foot to stop the ball hitting the fence.
3. Players must compete fairly and not cheat- coach can discuss the importance of honesty with the players.

Developments:

1. Players are split into two or three teams (depending on numbers). Players dribble through Greenhouses & keep individual score. Defenders anticipate which Greenhouses to defend by dribbling their ball & standing in the way, move quickly to defend other Greenhouses when needed.

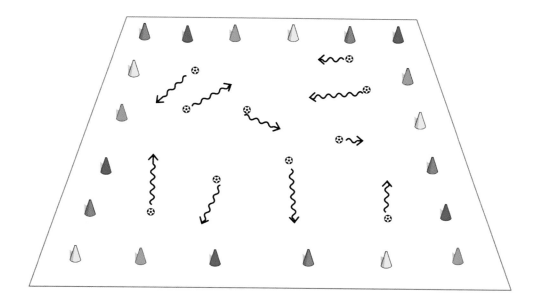

Easter – Shooting – Ball Mastery

We're going on an Easter Egg Hunt. We're going to use the Sole of the Foot just like a bunny does when they're hopping. Why do we need to master using the Sole of the Foot? Stop the ball. Why else might we use the sole of the foot? To tease and trick the defender.

Organisation:

1. Footballs 2. Goals 3. Bibs 4. 20 WH Cones 5. Golden Egg (Trophy, Chocolate – Something to hide under a WH Cone)

Story/Description: Players dribble around coach shouts out ball move, gives demo and players repeat.

1. Players are bunnies. 'Let's Hop'- Bunnies quickly toe-tap the top of the ball with alternating feet.
2. 'Wrap your Egg'- Sole of the foot on the ball & roll it forwards-backwards or outside-inside.
3. 'Crack your Egg'- 'Drop and Stop' the ball cracking it with the sole.
4. 'Protect your Egg'- If Players see the coach coming they must put their foot on top of the ball to protect it.
5. 'Eat your Egg'- Use both feet – Pass ball between feet.

Coaching Points:

1. Players attempt to use both feet whilst dribbling around the area.

Developments:

1. Challenge some players to protect the ball by stopping it with the sole of their foot and turning to dribble in a different direction.

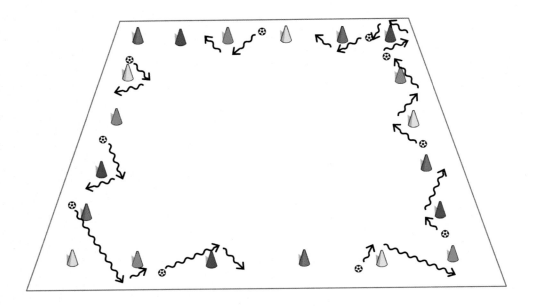

Easter – Shooting – Technique

We're going on an Easter Egg Hunt and we'll need to be able to shoot to search for the Golden Egg. Why is it important we learn to shoot accurately? So, we can score goals.

Organisation:

1. Footballs 2. Goals 3. Bibs 4. 20 WH Cones 5. Golden Egg (Trophy, Chocolate – Something to hide under a WH Cone)

Story/Description:

1. Players dribble in & out of the cones- lay out in a square.
2. Coach shouts 'Stop' & players attempt to stop immediately. They can shoot down the nearest cone to them and see if the Golden egg is there.
3. If it isn't they pick it up and wait to see if anyone else won.
4. If it is, they are the winner, everyone else closes their eyes and winner hides it and runs back to their ball.

Coaching Points:

1. Keep the ball close.
2. Stop it with sole of foot and return to square if you lose control of the ball.
3. Stop ball with sole of foot before shooting.

Developments:

1. Coach can ask certain players to shoot whilst ball is still rolling.

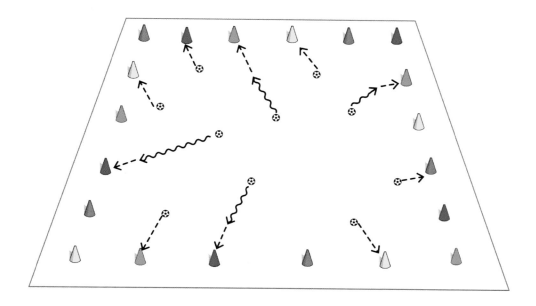

Easter – Shooting – Skill

We're going on an Easter Egg Hunt and we'll need to be able to shoot to search for the Golden Egg. Why is it important we learn to shoot accurately? So, we can score goals.

Organisation:

1. Footballs 2. Goals 3. Bibs 4. 20 WH Cones 5. Golden Egg (Trophy, Chocolate – Something to hide under a WH Cone)

Story/Description:

1. Players dribble inside area of the cones- Avoid bumping into other Easter Bunnies.
2. Coach shouts 'Golden Egg'.
3. Players shoot down any cone and see if the Golden egg is there.
4. If it isn't they pick it up and wait to see if anyone else won.
5. If it is, they are the winner, everyone else closes their eyes and winner hides it and runs back to their ball.

Coaching Points:

1. Keep the ball close.
2. Stop it with sole of foot and return to square if you lose control of the ball.
3. Stop ball with sole of foot before shooting.

Developments:

1. 1st Player to win loses their ball because they know where the Golden Egg is hidden. They have the option of tackling another bunny and taking their ball or they can attempt to protect the Golden Egg.

Firefighters – Turning & Tricks – Ball Mastery

This game is all about Firefighters, Firefighters are extraordinary people who are very brave and really strong. We will be working on Turning & Tricks. Why do we need to Turn? Protect the ball. Why do we need to do Tricks? Beat a Defender.

Organisation:

1. Footballs 2. Goals 3. Bibs 4. 11 Red Cones

Story/Description:

1. The Players are going through Firefighter's Training with a ball each.
2. The Captain (coach) shouts instructions and the Firefighters (players) perform the training drill.
3. 'Climb the Ladders' – Toe Taps (Fast & Light). 'FIREEEEE' – Roll Ball. 'Search & Rescue' – Step Overs. 'CPR' – Squeeze down on ball with sole.

Coaching Points:

1. Keep head up, don't bump into other Firefighters.
2. Keep arms up and out when rolling the ball.
3. Firefighters are very fit- so make it clear this game must be performed to the best of our abilities.

Developments:

1. Encourage small touches to maximize speed and control when Captain ask the firefighters to perform a training drill.

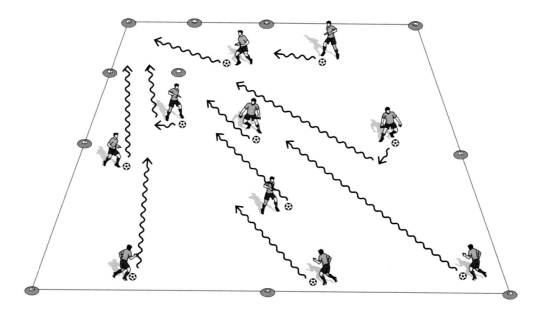

Firefighters – Turning & Tricks – Technique

This game is all about Firefighters, Firefighters are extraordinary people who are very brave and really strong. We will be working on Turning & Tricks. Why do we need to Turn? Protect the ball. Why do we need to do Tricks? Beat a Defender.

Organisation:

1. Footballs 2. Goals 3. Bibs 4. 11 Red Cones

Story/Description:

1. The Firefighters are driving the Fire Truck. They drive around the area avoiding collisions.
2. When the Coach shouts 'FIREEEEE', all the Firefighters must drive to the meeting point (Red Square). Coach should count down 5,4,3,2,1.
3. If they don't make it in time the firefighter must pick up their ball which is now on fire and drop, stop and roll it.

Coaching Points:

1. Keep the ball under control and close
2. Change of speed and/or direction.

Developments:

1. Add a task once the player arrives to the meeting point, i.e., toe taps, a dribbling move, etc.

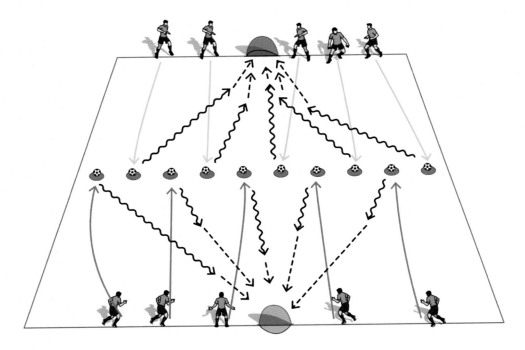

Firefighters – Turning & Tricks – Skill

This game is all about Firefighters, Firefighters are extraordinary people who are very brave and really strong. We will be working on Turning & Tricks. Why do we need to Turn? Protect the ball. Why do we need to do Tricks? Beat a Defender.

Organisation:

1. Footballs 2. Goals 3. Bibs 4. 11 Red Cones

Story/Description: Bucket Brigade - Firefighters must be physically fit but they like to have fun too.

1. 2 Teams at opposite ends of the area. 1 goal placed on each end line and all footballs lined up in the middle.
2. Players race to collect the little buckets of water (Footballs) and kick them in their team's big bucket (net). Finish by counting each team's collection & declare the winning team.
3. 3. Next, they are going to kick the buckets of water at the other firefighters- try to get fewer footballs on your side than the other team. Play for a couple of minutes and count footballs.

Coaching Points:

1. Keep football close so you can shoot early & accurately
2. Lift head early to assess which football to take and if it goes before you get there do you know where the other options are.

Developments:

1. Players can only shoot with their 'other' foot.
2. Players must only dribble it in or shoot within touches.

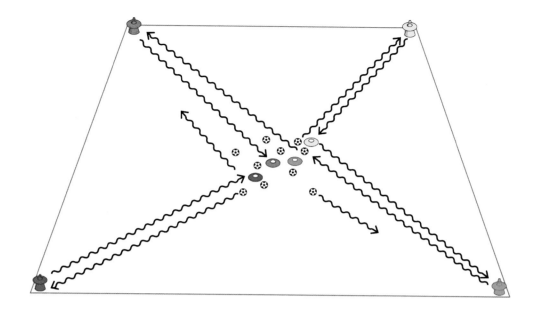

The Queen's Birthday – Turning & Shooting – Ball Mastery

This game is about The Queen's Birthday. We will be working on Turning & also shooting. Why do we need to Turn? Protect the ball. Why is it important to shoot accurately? So, we can score goals.

Organisation:

1. Footballs 2. Goals 3. Bibs 4. 1 Red, Yellow, Blue & Green WH Cone. 10/15 Red, Yellow, Blue & Green Cones.

Story/Description:

1. The Players are shopping for party items. They dribble to each corner shop, collect an item and place it in the middle at home. Red- Fireworks, Blue- Chocolate, Green- Party Hats, Yellow- Gift.
2. Place the bottom two WH Cones up at the top so all 4 cones are on the same line with an equal distance between each one. Players will now organise items at home by re-placing them back on the corresponding cone; Blue to Blue.

Coaching Points:

1. When turning around make sure ball is in control and don't bump into other players. Use sole of the foot to stop the ball at the cones.

Developments:

1. Ask players to collect a party hat (Green Cone) whilst dribbling around the room try to keep it balanced on their head.
2. Ask players to collect a Firework (Red Cone) find space pick up ball & throw it up, control it on the way down or catch it as high as possible like a Goalkeeper.

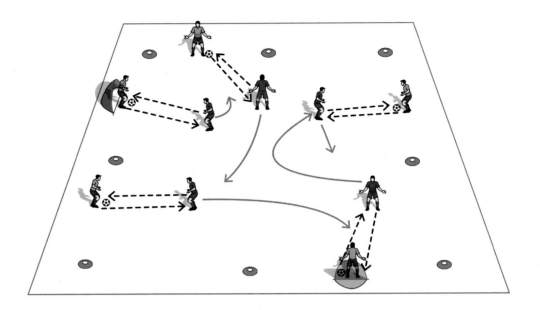

The Queen's Birthday – Turning & Shooting – Technique

This game is about The Queen's Birthday. We will be working on Turning & also shooting. Why do we need to Turn? Protect the ball. Why is it important to shoot accurately? So, we can score goals.

Organisation:

1. Footballs 2. Goals 3. Bibs 4. 1 Red, Yellow, Blue & Green WH Cone. 10/15 Red, Yellow, Blue & Green Cones.

Story/Description:

1. The Players are playing pass the parcel for the Queen's Birthday. Set up a square. Players on the outside start with a ball. Remaining players start in the middle without a ball.
2. Move towards the players on the outside & return pass. Players can shoot against Goalkeepers.

Coaching Points:

1. Look for the free player when on the move & communicate before receiving the ball with eyes and speech.
2. Pass the ball with one touch, with the right speed, at the right time.
3. Shoot into the corners or the most open part of the goal.

Developments:

1. Start by halving the players on the inside and outside. If it's too easy you can remove an outside player(s) & put them in the middle & then coach the delay/hastening of movement to receive the ball. If it's too difficult add an outside player so that there is always a free player to get the ball from.

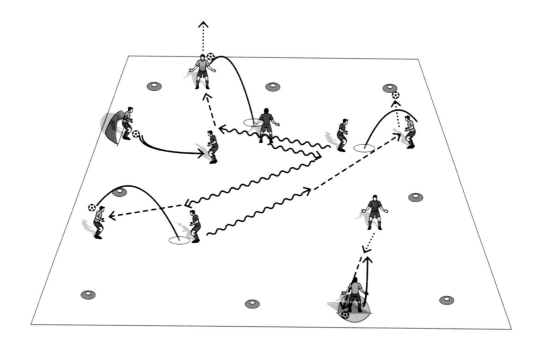

The Queen's Birthday – Turning & Shooting – Skill

This game is about The Queen's Birthday. We will be working on Turning & also shooting. Why do we need to Turn? Protect the ball. Why is it important to shoot accurately? So, we can score goals.

Organisation:

1. Footballs 2. Goals 3. Bibs 4. 1 Red, Yellow, Blue & Green WH Cone. 10/15 Red, Yellow, Blue & Green Cones.

Story/Description:

1. The Players are setting off the Fireworks we bought earlier. Players on the outside throw-in the Fireworks (Football) to inside players who check the fireworks are safe. They turn & find a 'Free' outside player & shoot the ball into them; outside players then set the fireworks off by throwing them up in the air and catching the ball as high possible like a goalkeeper.
2. When the Goalkeepers save the ball with their feet they should pass the ball to the next player they encounter, if they catch the ball they should roll the ball to the player. Goalkeepers diffuse fireworks by keeping it tight to the body.

Coaching Points:

1. Demo overhead throw-in's let mistakes happen initially but correct technique if it continues.

Developments:

1. U4's throw ball in underarm/overhead & players play it straight back in. U5's/U6's should prepare for matches via practicing overhead throw-ins.
2. Try to control the throw-in before it bounces with different parts of the body/foot also.

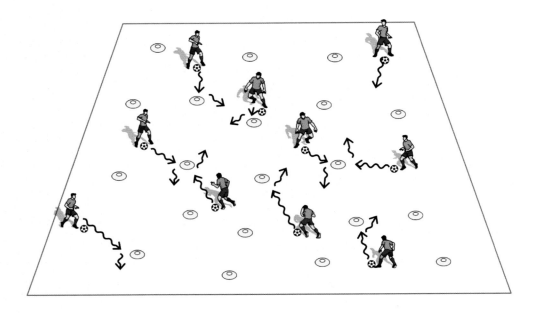

Galaxy Combat – Moving Left & Right – Ball Mastery

This game is all about Galaxy Combat. We will be focusing on moving Left & Right, so we can beat the Galactic Soldiers. Why is it important to move Left & Right in football? To trick Defenders.

Organisation:

1. Footballs 2. Goals 3. Bibs 4. 20 White Cones

Story/Description: A long time ago in a galaxy far, far away!

1. The Coach is Master Knight and they are teaching the Knights (Players) how to defeat the Galactic Soldiers. Knights know how to move left & right out of danger quickly.
2. Coach lays out 20 White Cones (Galactic Soldiers).
3. Players dribble at the Galactic Soldiers but at the last second move quickly to the left or right.

Coaching Points:

1. When attacking the Galactic Soldiers show players how to use the inside of the foot to drag it past the cones.
2. Show players how to use the outside of the foot to move left/right past the cones.

Developments:

1. Can Knights use a trick to get past the Galactic Soldiers e.g. Step-over, stop-push, V turn.

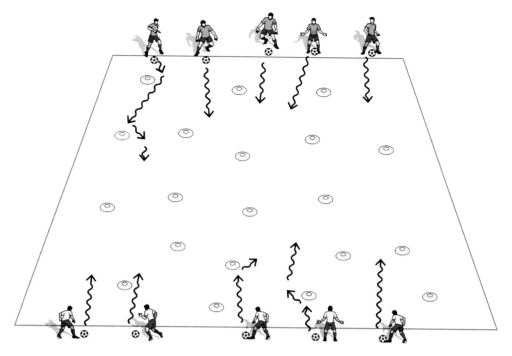

Galaxy Combat – Moving Left & Right – Technique

This game is all about Galaxy Combat. We will be focusing on moving Left & Right, so we can beat the Galactic Soldiers. Why is it important to move Left & Right in football? To trick Defenders.

Organisation:

1. Footballs 2. Goals 3. Bibs 4. 20 White Cones

Story/Description: Knights Vs. Galactic Soldiers.

1. Split players into two teams and separate to other ends of the area. One team with bibs.
2. Galactic Soldiers attack the Knights and Vice Versa.
3. Players dribble towards each other and move left and right avoiding attacks.
4. Be careful of the cones and avoid these moving left and right.

Coaching Points:

1. Players keep their eyes up to check for players approaching, avoid collisions and to see the ever-changing picture.
2. Small touches makes it easier to move left and right quick.

Developments:

1. Players can try to kick opponent's ball away whilst protecting their own.

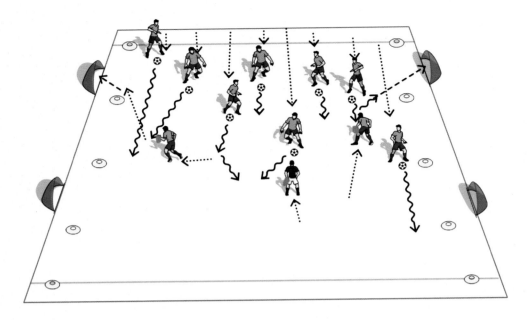

Galaxy Combat – Moving Left & Right – Skill

This game is all about Galaxy Combat. We will be focusing on moving Left & Right, so we can beat the Galactic Soldiers. Why is it important to move Left & Right in football? To trick Defenders.

Organisation:

1. Footballs 2. Goals 3. Bibs 4. 20 White Cones

Story/Description: Knights Vs. Galactic Soldiers.

1. The coach places nets at the side and 2 lines of cones down the sides to create a middle area.
2. Master Knight (Coach) and 2 Knights (Players) are going to take on the Galactic Soldiers.
3. They hold their Light Swords (Bibs) in their hands and try to kick the Galactic Soldiers football out of the galaxy.
4. If the Galactic Soldiers ball is kicked out of the galaxy, they become a Knight. They collect a bib and help Master Knight and the Knights.

Coaching Points:

1. Look for opportunities to get past the Knights for e.g. when they are trying to get another Galactic Soldier.
2. Can you help a Galactic Soldier in trouble out by dribbling towards a Knight and distracting them. This is a good opportunity to build on teamwork.

Developments:

1. Knights must now kick the footballs into the nets at the side and not just out of the area. This gives the Galactic Soldiers an opportunity to win their ball back.

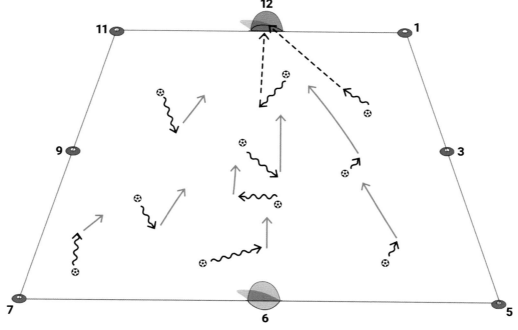

© Copyright www.academysoccercoach.co.uk 2018

What Time Is It? – Moving Forward & Stopping – Ball Mastery

Our game is all about The Time. We will be working on moving forward with the ball and stopping. Keeping the ball under control with both feet, they move forward quickly, and they learn to stop immediately, players can use the sole of the foot to stop the football rolling.

Organisation:

1. Footballs 2. Goals 3. Bibs 4. 6 Blue Cones

Story/Description:

1. The Coach is the Timekeeper.
2. The Players dribble around the Clock.
3. When the Timekeeper shouts a time, they must shoot into the time zone (net) or dribble and wait at the right time e.g. 12 o'clock players dribble and shoot.

Coaching Points:

1. Players attempt to use both feet whilst dribbling around the clock.
2. Coach timing of stopping and re-moving forward.

Developments:

1. To extend play; Timekeepers can shout out 2 times e.g. 1 o'clock and then 6 o'clock.

35

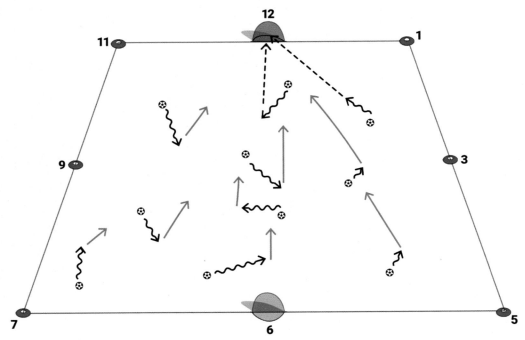

© Copyright www.academysoccercoach.co.uk 2018

What Time Is It? – Moving Forward & Stopping – Technique

Our game is all about The Time. We will be working on moving forward with the ball and stopping.

Organisation:

1. Footballs 2. Goals 3. Bibs 4. 6 Blue Cones

Story/Description: The Coach is the Timekeeper. The Players dribble around the Clock. The Timekeeper shout's a time & an action. Players dribble to the time & perform the action.

1. 1 o'clock; Protect your lunch – Keep your football safe whilst trying to kick other footballs away.
   3 o'clock; Drop off your school bag – Drop & Stop the ball 3 times, alternating feet.
   5 o'clock; Let's Bake & Shake the mix – Pass ball between Left & Right foot.
   6 o'clock; GOAL – Shoot at the goal.
   7 o'clock; Walk the dog – Dribble forward and then 'Stop' whilst the dog sniffs the trees.
   9 o'clock; Up the stairs for bed – 20 Toe Taps.
   11 o'clock; Roll over for Sweet Dreams – Roll ball with sole 10 times with each foot.
   12 o'clock; GOAL – Shoot at the goal.

Coaching Points:

1. Players attempt to use both feet whilst dribbling around the clock.
2. Coach timing of stopping and re-moving forward.

Developments:

1. To extend play; Timekeepers can shout out 2 times e.g. 1 o'clock and then 6 o'clock.

CHRIS HUGHES

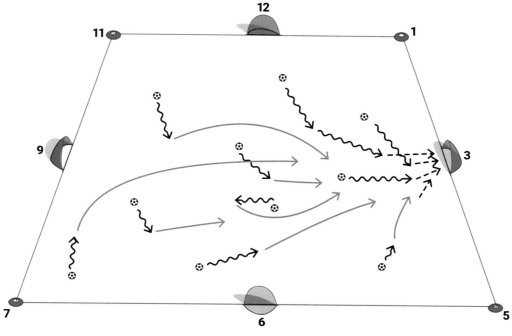

© Copyright www.academysoccercoach.co.uk 2018

What Time Is It? – Moving Forward & Stopping – Skill

Our game is all about The Time. We will be working on moving forward with the ball and stopping. Keeping the ball under control with both feet, they move forward quickly, and they learn to stop immediately, players can use the sole of the foot to stop the football rolling.

Organisation:

1. Footballs 2. Goals 3. Bibs 4. 6 Blue Cones

Story/Description: The Coach is the Timekeeper. The Players dribble around the Clock. The Timekeeper shout's a time & players aim to be the quickest to score.

1. 3 o'clock; GOAL – Shoot at the goal.
    6 o'clock; GOAL – Shoot at the goal.
    9 o'clock; GOAL – Shoot at the goal.
    12 o'clock; GOAL – Shoot at the goal.

Coaching Points:

1. Keep the football close so they can stop & turn as soon as they hear the command.
2. Timing of shot and the weight needed i.e. don't hit somebody else or shoot to soft/hard.

Developments:

1. To extend play; Timekeepers can split players up into 4 and start behind a goal. Timekeeper rolls a ball in and calls out which goal should be scored in i.e. 3 o'clock, One player from each team competes in a 4x1 situation.

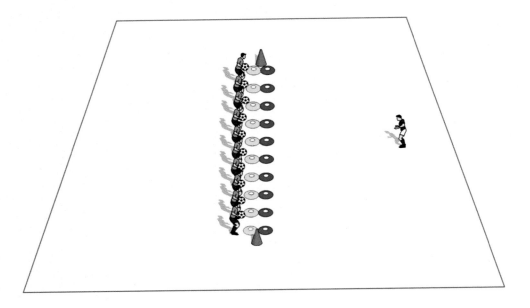

Battleships – Controlling the ball with both feet & Shooting – Ball Mastery

This game is all about Battleships. We will be working on controlling the ball with both feet & working on some Shooting too.

Organisation:

1. Footballs 2. Goals 3. Bibs 4. 10 Blue & Yellow Cones 5. 20 WH Cones

Story/Description:

1. All Players start with a ball in their hand standing on the sand facing the coach.
2. When the coach shouts out 'In the Sea' all players must jump over the Yellow cones and land on the blue side- The Sea.
3. When the coach shouts out 'On the Sand' all the players jump away from the coach back over the cones onto the sand.
4. The coach attempts to trick the players by quickly changing commands i.e. On the Sand, In the Sea, In the Sea, On the Sand.
5. If a player jumps in the wrong direction, they join the coach.
6. Play for a couple of minutes and see how many players you can catch out.

Coaching Points:

1. Feet together when jumping
2. Arms out to balance
3. Listen carefully.

Developments:

1. Allow the first player out to deliver commands until they catch somebody and rotate.

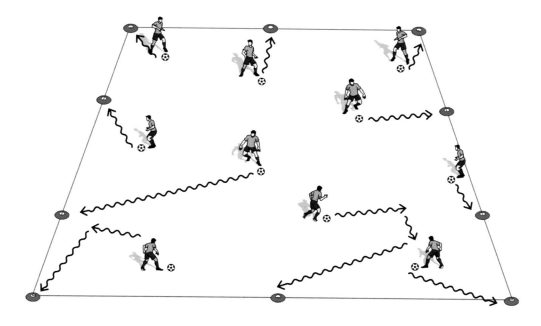

Battleships – Controlling the ball with both feet & Shooting – Technique

This game is all about Battleships. We will be working on controlling the ball with both feet & working on some Shooting too.

Organisation:

1. Footballs 2. Goals 3. Bibs 4. 10 Blue & Yellow Cones 5. 20 WH Cones

Story/Description:

1. Players are preparing for battle. They dribble around the Battleship.
2. When the coach shouts 'SEATS' they must dribble and find an empty seat (Blue Cone).
3. Remove a Seat and have one less than the number of players to introduce competition.

Coaching Points:

1. Use both feet when dribbling to move and change direction quickly
2. Keep head up and listen to command
3. Ability to choose best suited seat and then get there quickly and ability to move on if they one is taken before you get there.

Developments:

1. Remove another seat to increase competition.

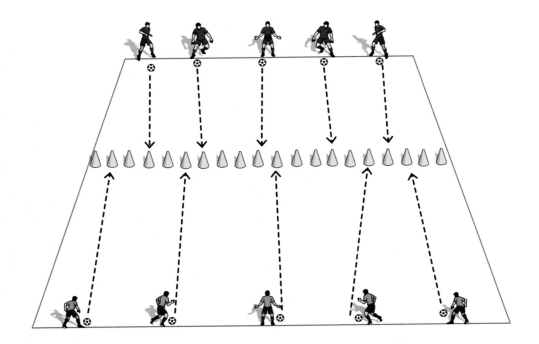

Battleships – Controlling the ball with both feet & Shooting – Skill

This game is all about Battleships. We will be working on controlling the ball with both feet & working on some Shooting too.

Organisation:

1. Footballs 2. Goals 3. Bibs 4. 10 Blue & Yellow Cones 5. 20 WH Cones

Story/Description:

1. Players split into 2 teams and have a ball each.
2. The players are firing their missiles (Footballs) at the Battleships (WH Cones).
3. Coach can shout commands to interrupt the battle, start by shouting; 'Destroy the Battleships'.

- 'Reload the missiles' – Retrieve footballs.
- 'Repair the Battleships' – Put WH Cones back upright.
- 'Enemy planes are coming' – The players shield their ball from the coach.
- 'Destroy the enemy planes' – Player shoot to hit the coach.

Coaching Points:

1. Use the inside of foot when shooting for better accuracy.

Developments:

1. During Small Sided Game use WH Cones instead of Goals and aim to knock them over to score.

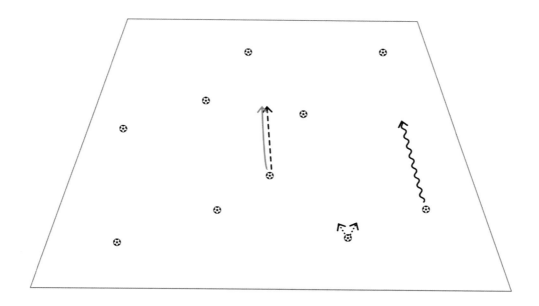

Camping – Shooting – Ball Mastery

This game is all about Camping. We'll be focusing on shooting. Why is it important we learn to shoot accurately? So, we can score goals & you need to score goals to win games.

Organisation:

1. Footballs 2. Goals 3. Bibs 4. WH Cones

Story/Description:

1. Players dribble around the campsite. Coach shouts actions and demos in order.
2. 'Nail down the tent' – Throw football up in the air, when it drops stop it with sole of the foot.
3. 'Blow up the air bed' – Pump knee's whilst doing Toe Taps on the football.
4. 'Roll out the sleeping bag' – Roll ball with sole of foot in V shape.
5. 'It's Windy' – Kick ball out in front, chase it & stop it with the sole of the foot.
6. 'Step over the slugs' – Players dribble & practise Step-Overs.
7. 'RAAAIN' – Drop & protect the ball like a Goalkeeper. Shout this action at any point & on numerous occasions.

Coaching Points:

1. When dropping the ball, tell the players it's ok if the football bounces a couple of times but try to stop it as quick as they can.
2. Ensure correct technique is being used when doing V shape turns.

Developments:

1. Don't let the football bounce when dropping it, try to bring it down with the top of their foot.

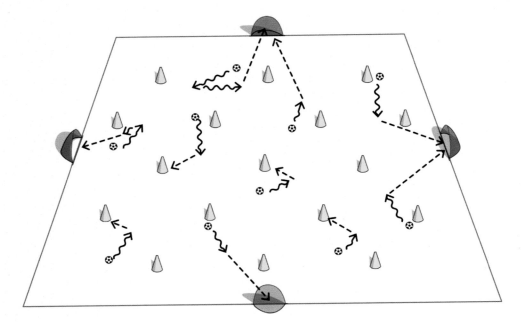

Camping – Shooting – Technique

This game is all about Camping. We'll be focusing on shooting. Why is it important we learn to shoot accurately? So, we can score goals & you need to score goals to win games.

Organisation:

1. Footballs 2. Goals 3. Bibs 4. WH Cones.

Story/Description:

1. Players dribble around the campsite avoiding the Witch Hat Cones (Tents).
2. Coach shouts 'RAIN' players must find shelter by shooting into the goals.
3. Coach shouts 'It's Windy' players attempt to knock down the Tents.

Coaching Points:

1. Coach the detail between shooting with Power or Accuracy. Explain that there are times when one of them is more suitable (Distance to goal, Goalkeepers position etc.)

Developments:

1. Introduce countdown to score, 3,2,1. 2. Challenge players to dribble around a tent before shooting into Tents.

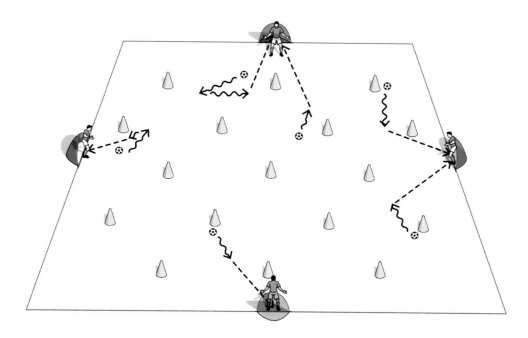

Camping – Shooting – Skill

This game is all about Camping. We'll be focusing on shooting. Why is it important we learn to shoot accurately? So, we can score goals & you need to score goals to win games.

Organisation:

1. Footballs 2. Goals 3. Bibs 4. WH Cones.

Story/Description:

1. Place 4 Goalkeepers in the nets.
2. Players dribble around the campsite avoiding the Witch Hat Cones (Tents).
3. Coach shouts 'RAIN' players must find shelter by shooting into the goals.
4. Coach shouts 'It's Windy' players attempt to knock down the Tents.

Coaching Points:

1. Watch for players making the wrong decision (power/accuracy) and drop in to remind them 1-2-1 of the options then can try.
2. Explain to players that if a GK is already facing a shot to turn and find another net to shoot at.

Developments:

1. If player misses a shot then they swop & become the GK.

What's Next?

Matches; lots and lots of matches!

Have you read our other books?

In addition to The Spring Series we have The Winter Series, The Summer Series, The Autumn Series and The All Seasons Series.

U7's-U11's Foundation Phase

I recommend visiting this website and buying this book.

The Football Syllabus - Foundation Phase Syllabus

"Featuring a fully comprehensive 36-week Coaching Syllabus, with your players development at the centre. The Syllabus provides coaches with a step by step guide to deliver an in-depth, structured 36-week syllabus with over 100 practises."

The Foundation Phase Syllabus also boasts additional support with expert advice on how to manage difference and behaviour, coaching styles, how to deliver a match day... and more!

Unrivalled personal support comes as standard."

www.thefootballsyllabus.co.uk

Academy Soccer Coach

All session diagrams created with the Session Template Software™ at academysoccercoach. co.uk.

Secret Marketing Strategy

If you're searching for something a bit different for your next Soccer School or Grassroots Club leaflet design, then my die-cut, football shirt flyers are the ideal way to stand out and get noticed.

My printing team can design and develop a range of styles to give you plenty of choices – Hoops, Stripes, Sashes, Checkers or Solid kits all with personalisation and excellent quality part of the service... We will also supply a JPEG which you can upload to all your social media platforms too!

To create an effective soccer school marketing strategy, you need to stand out from the crowd – and with so much competition for local grassroots clubs, this head-turning design is essential.

While leaflet campaigns are a great low-cost, low-hassle way of advertising your business to the local marketplace, with so many other children's activity providers doing the same thing, you need to make sure your leaflet gets put to the top of the pile.

Because I've been providing marketing supplies and support to grassroots clubs for over 10 years, I've learned a thing or two about what kind of marketing gets the best results.

The bulk of flyers and leaflets distributed by children's activity and sport providers tend to be the standard square or rectangular shape, but I've found that a shaped leaflet design adds a whole new dimension to your strategy. By doing things differently, your leaflets will get noticed and your club will be remembered – and it shows that your club is anything but standard!

Our football shirt leaflets can be used in conjunction with any of our general designs, and we can tailor various elements to make the finished product even more personal to your club, such as:

- Your club logo
- Your contact details
- Your location
- Your message

By their very nature, these leaflets are a little more restrictive when it comes to space for content, so the focus needs to be on a clear, concise and engaging message.

With my commitment to ensuring high quality and the more intricate nature of the design, these leaflets take a little longer to produce, making them slightly higher in cost.

The overall cost comes in at around just 10% more than a standard leaflet. However, once you've taken these into all your local schools. The extra impact they make will soon see them paying for themselves! 300 Double-Sided Leaflets including design, print, cut and free delivery will cost £100.

To order your double-sided football shirt leaflets we will need you to complete a design requirement order form on our website if you have any issues or want to discuss your design with genuine industry experts give us a call on 07792715495 and we'll be happy to answer any questions you have. To complete the form please visit www.littlelegendsuk.co.uk/shop

SALFORD STORM FC

RECEPTION

PLAYERS WANTED

UNDER **5** 'S

OUR UNDER 5 TEAM IS RECRUITING
PLAYERS TO ADD TO THEIR SQUAD.

IF ANY BOYS OR GIRLS IN RECEPTION
WOULD LIKE TO JOIN OUR CLUB AND
TRAIN WITH FA QUALIFIED COACHES,

CONTACT CHRIS ON 07792 715495
OR VISIT WWW.LITTLELEGENDSUK.CO.UK

TRAINING SESSIONS:
THE EMMANUEL CHURCH & CENTRE
174 LANGWORTHY ROAD, M6 5PN.
SATURDAY MORNINGS 9-10 OR 10-11.

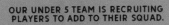

About the Author

I started coaching when I was 16 years old and have coached players from 18 months old to adults. I've always coached children from 18 months to 6 but during this time I have also coached for Manchester United FC and Bolton Wanderers with players aged from 8 to 18 years old. I decided during this time that I would focus on our youngest players and learn as much as I could about children in this age range and how they learn and how I think we should teach them. I didn't plan on writing a book initially but after taking my cousin – Charlie - who was 5 at the time to various different junior clubs, I witnessed a whole host of sessions that were totally inappropriate for that age group and so I decided that I would compile a list of sessions and write a book. I watched him "attempt" at just 5 years old; laps of the pitch, press-ups, squats, sit-ups, practice throw-ins and the standard passing line drill where there is 1 ball between 12 players. It was at this moment I realised that these coaches needed help. I spoke to one of the coaches after the session to see if he needed a hand and explained that I was Charlie's cousin, he was so grateful and explained that he had never coached U5's before but because nobody else would do it, this dad decided to step up and take on the role. If only there was somewhere, he could have found help!

My dream for this series of books is to transform U5 & U6's football coaching sessions worldwide. My vision for the series is its ability to empower the coaches within this age group. I want too successfully inspire, teach, train, coach, mentor and guide my newly empowered coaches to grow an army of technically competent skilled footballers who love the game and for each and every coach to become a master of U5 and U6's coaching.

I'm delighted to release these books and to assist the thousands of U5's & U6's coaches out there!

Printed in the United States
By Bookmasters